Defeathering the INDIAN

"Not fossilized, unadaptive, not sealed into the past, but plastic, adaptive, assimilative..."

John Collier, *Indians of the Americas*

"*Defeathering the Indian*... written out of a sincere desire to reduce the psychological violence done to Native students in our education system."

Owen Haythorne, Co-ordinator,
Native Curriculum Resource Project

A Handbook on Native Studies
Originated under the Auspices
of the
Alberta Department of Education

Defeathering the INDIAN

EMMA LaROQUE

The Book Society of Canada Limited   *Agincourt, Canada*

Copyright © The Book Society of Canada Limited, 1975
In association with the Alberta Department of Education

Photo Credits:
Courtesy of the Alberta Native Communications Society, Edmonton, Alberta, ii, 3, 9, 12, 16, 20, 21, 25, 28, 35, 38, 42, 45, 51, 55, 60, 61, 63, 66, 69; Federal Department of Indian Affairs and Northern Development, 70; Donovan Clemson from Miller Services, Toronto, 75; Richard Harrington from Miller Services, Toronto, ix. Cover photograph (lower) courtesy of Floyd Elliott.
Every reasonable effort has been made to trace ownership and copyright of all photographs used in this text. Information will be welcomed which will enable the publisher to rectify any reference in a future printing.

It is an infringement of the author's rights and a violation of the Copyright Law to reproduce or utilize in any form or by any means, electronic or mechanical, including photocopying, electrostatic copying, recording or by any information storage and retrieval system or any other way passages from this book without the written permission of the publishers.

ISBN 0-7725-5028-X
Cover design: Brant Cowie / Artplus
Printed in Canada
1 2 3 4 5 6 7 80 79 78 77 76 75

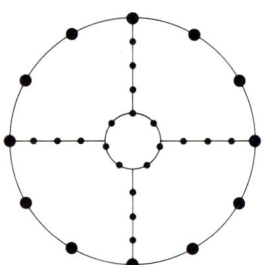

This simple circle, representing the sacred Medicine Wheel of the Plains Indians, symbolizes a wholistic world-view shared by many Native people.

In Appreciation

I wish to thank various members of the Alberta Department of Education, especially Dr. Harry Sherk, Associate Director of Curriculum responsible for Social Studies. Without his initial efforts this project would not have been possible. I also thank Dr. E.A. Torgunrud, Director of Curriculum, for his interest and encouragement throughout.

I am grateful to Ms. Anita Jenkins, Curriculum Editor, for her careful corrections of the manuscript. Thanks also to Mrs. Carol Roth for proof-reading part of the manuscript.

I especially valued the help from the other members of our Native Curriculum Resource Project: Mrs. Carol Layton and Mr. Owen Haythorne. They often took time to listen to my woes regarding the manuscript and shared their insights to help me on. Beyond this, I appreciated their sense of humor in times of dire stress, and their friendship. A special word must be said for Mr. Haythorne, co-ordinator of the project, who spent many hours discussing, debating and clarifying with me the contents of this handbook.

Sometimes we take our friends for granted during special projects. I heartily thank mine for their support, helpful suggestions and many a hot cup of coffee.

Finally, I dedicate this handbook to my family; my parents, my sister and her lovely family, my two brothers and their young families. These very dear people's lives and struggles, and their love for me have shaped my life and profoundly influenced my thinking as well as the direction and nature of my concerns and personal convictions.

Emma LaRoque

Contents

In Appreciation v
Acknowledgements viii
Introduction x

Chapter 1 **RATIONALE** *1*

Chapter 2 **HERITAGE OR CULTURE?** *7*
In the Context of the Classroom:
    Native people must define themselves *13*
    Educators must not confuse present Indian culture with
       heritage *14*
    Culture is more than a package of tangibles *23*

Chapter 3 **STEREOTYPES: PAST AND PRESENT** *31*
The various stereotyped images of Native people *32*
In the Context of the Classroom:
    Preparing lessons on stereotyping *44*
    Preparing lessons on how cultures clash *46*

Chapter 4 **THE MEDIA AND THE INDIAN** *49*
The printed word, language, and pictures *50*
In the Context of the Classroom:
    About history books *62*
    About compensatory education *65*
    A personal essay on poverty *67*
    Beyond words *71*

Chapter 5 **MISCELLANEOUS REFLECTIONS** *73*

Footnotes 79
Recommendations for Further Reading 81

Acknowledgements

Reprinted by permission of Doubleday (Canada) Limited: material from *Agouhanna* by Claude Aubry; copyright © 1972 by Doubleday (Canada) Limited (Toronto). Holt, Rinehart & Winston: For material from *Bury My Heart At Wounded Knee* by Dee Brown; copyright © 1970 by Holt, Rinehart & Winston (New York); for material from *Compensatory Education for Cultural Deprivation* by Benjamin S. Bloom and others; copyright © 1968 by Holt, Rinehart & Winston (New York). Reprinted by permission of The Canadian Publishers, McClelland and Stewart Limited (Toronto): material from *Without Reserve* by Sheila Burnford; copyright © 1969 by McClelland and Stewart Limited. New American Library, Inc.: For material from *Indians of the Americas* by John Collier; copyright © 1947 by New American Library, Inc. (New York). Ontario Institute for Studies in Education: For material from *Teaching Prejudice* by Garnet McDiarmid and David Pratt; copyright © 1971 by Ontario Institute for Studies in Education (Toronto).

Every reasonable effort has been made to trace ownership of copyright material. Information will be welcomed which will enable the publisher to rectify any reference in a future printing.

Psychological violence. What is it? What are the implications for our present educational system?

Introduction

In the 1960's a new hope began to dawn for Native people; agents of the dominant society actually began to listen to them. The change was slow at first, but by the beginning of the 1970's the process was gathering momentum. The historic "White Paper" of 1969 provided a catalyst for strong and concerted reactions from Native groups across the country. Alberta's *Citizens Plus* and Harold Cardinal's *The Unjust Society* set the tone for Native expression.

Following the debate on general policies represented by the above documents, statements on specific concerns began to surface in the form of briefs and policy papers all across Canada. In education the most significant was *Indian Control of Education* prepared by the National Indian Brotherhood in 1972 and eventually accepted in its entirety by the then Minister of Indian Affairs, the Hon. Jean Chretien.

While organized groups of Native people were seizing the opportunity to be heard in a previously callous and deaf society, individual Native people struggled to find identity and relevance in a confusing world. One of these individuals was Emma LaRoque. To know Emma's struggles is to know the struggles of a people. To learn about Emma's interrelationship with the dominant society and its institution, the school, is to learn about what directions we as educators (or students) might pursue as we undertake Native Studies programs. Although *Defeathering the Indian* is a commentary on education based on personal experiences, some further background may be helpful in establishing a perspective.

Born twenty-five years ago in a one-roomed, kerosene-lit, mud-plastered log cabin in the middle of winter in northeastern Alberta, Emma began her life in the Cree-Métis culture of that era. Her great-grandfather had been a buffalo hunter and scout in the Métis Red River settlements in Manitoba. Later her grandfather was a voyageur-guide on the York boats on the Athabasca River. Although her ancestors were key figures in the Western Canadian society of their time, by the time Emma was born her people had been pushed into semi-isolation by the mainstream of society. However, in spite of the insecurity of being squatters on the land, and despite the threat of diseases such as tuberculosis, and the alienation from other groups of Canadians, Emma's family had retained elements of spiritual stability and relevance guided by the wisdom of Cree legend and mythology. (See "A Personal Essay on Poverty", p. 67)

From this background Emma entered school at the age of nine. As one of the first Métis children in isolated communities to attend school in any systematic way, Emma met teachers and a curriculum which did everything but "start where the child is". In *Defeathering the Indian* Emma's recollections of her school experiences provide vivid evidence of their effect on her search for personhood. From Big Bay (or Barnegat) to Owl River, to Lac-la-Biche, to Anzac, to Three Hills, Emma completed twelve years of basic education in ten in spite of the fact that her first language was Cree and despite the dehumanizing experiences recounted in this handbook.

Emma was lucky; she possessed a superior ability to perform the intellectual tasks expected at school. This ability kept her at or near the top of the class and provided her with a sense of worth even in an alien world. In Grade 8, receiving a Northland achievement pin was apparently a formal recognition of her relevance to white society.

After high school Emma worked for six months as a ward-clerk in the Barrhead, Alberta, hospital. Later she worked as a counsellor for juvenile delinquents in summer camps before enrolling in the Faculty of Education at Camrose Lutheran College sixty miles east of Edmonton. Emma credits experiences in sociology classes there with giving her the opportunity to rediscover the remnants of her Indian heritage: "It was a time of discovery in leaps and bounds ... a time of much personal pain ... a time of anger and bitterness against oppression ... one of the more tumultuous moments of my life". However, in spite of it being a trying time, Emma was involved in student affairs for which she received a Service Award. After reading *Defeathering the Indian* anyone with any sensitivity at all will begin to appreciate why Emma's struggle was so difficult.

After two years at Camrose Emma joined the staff of the Alberta

Native Communications Society (ANCS) in 1971, first as a reporter, then as assistant editor for the newspaper *Native People*. With ANCS she helped develop and, later, became the co-ordinator of the Education Department of ANCS. Her first efforts in this role were directed towards producing Native-oriented, dramatized radio programs in cooperation with Alberta School Broadcasts.

In the fall of 1972 Miss LaRoque went to Goshen College in Goshen, Indiana, graduating in December 1973 with a B.A. in English/Communications. Again, Emma was involved, this time as a vice-president of the College's community government as well as serving on various committees. She also won the College's Annual Oratory Award. Between sessions in the summer of 1973 Miss LaRoque travelled extensively throughout the U.S. reporting on Native events in many areas such as the Choctaw reservation in Mississippi, the Navaho reservations in Arizona and New Mexico, and Wounded Knee in South Dakota. In addition, Emma has been a guest speaker or resource person in intercultural conventions and seminars in both Canada and the U.S.

Back in Edmonton in 1974, Emma spent four months as a script writer for ANCS before setting to work on *Defeathering the Indian*.*
Presently, she is enrolled in a Master of Divinity program in Indiana after receiving the prestigious Rockefeller Fellowship tenable at a theological school of her choice.

As a handbook for Native Studies, *Defeathering the Indian* provides a rare opportunity to view education through the eyes of a Native person. In writing this handbook, Emma has brought together her rich and varied experiences, from her semi-isolated home in northeastern Alberta to the most cosmopolitan cities of North America. Having lived in "both worlds" Emma sees valuable elements in each. What frustrates her is the lack of opportunity to learn about Native people and their world. As Emma so vividly and aptly points out in "A Personal Essay on Poverty", terms such as cultural depriva-

---

* Miss LaRoque was supported in her writing of this handbook by a S.T.E.P. grant (Summer Temporary Employment Project) sponsored by the Curriculum Branch, Department of Education, government of the Province of Alberta.

tion become meaningless when one knows and understands both cultures.

Some theorists would say that we are the product of our experiences. Others would say that what we will become is determined primarily by our earliest experiences. Since the question of Native values and their relevance to our modern society arises from time to time, let us consider Emma's values as they might be derived from her early family experiences: In Emma's words, her values include: "Bringing people together ... reconciliation ... service to humanity ... openness and honesty ... objection to war and violence ... respect for personhood ... opposition to imposition by one group on another ... ". Most of these values are evident in *Defeathering the Indian* because it has been written out of a sincere desire to reduce the psychological violence done to Native students in our education system. It does so with humour, with a sensitivity for the difficulties inherent in an educator's defined task, and with an authentic personal experience as its basis.

Defeathering the Indian should be useful to policy-makers at all levels, to administrators, to classroom teachers, to curriculum developers, to educators of teachers, and to Native organizations. It could be used as a resource for teacher in-service sessions or workshops, teacher education classes, and high school social studies classes, as well as provide invaluable insight for people in the media and a concerned public, generally. Crucial to any meaningful discussions about Native Studies programs are the issues raised by LaRoque: the problem of stereotypes, the ignorance of non-Natives about Native people, and the confusion between culture and heritage.

To those who are sincerely committed to providing a more relevant learning experience for Native students or to improving knowledge about Native people in all students and in Canadians, generally, I am sure that you will find *Defeathering the Indian* an enjoyable and rewarding experience. However, the ultimate value of this handbook will be determined by the extent to which the suggestions contained therein become a part of the reader's daily actions, attitudes and decisions relative to Native people.

Owen Haythorne, *Co-ordinator,*
Native Curriculum Resource Project

1
Rationale

Much has been said and written on education by and for Native people. There is a new surge of interest and effort among some schools and universities in Canada to bring about education relevant to Indian students. While these new endeavors cannot be minimized, it is this author's contention that education by and for Native people is not sufficient.

Statistically, Native students have not responded to the existing educational system. It is believed that lack of pride in Indianness has contributed greatly towards the failure rate. This is not surprising since Canadian schools have done precious little to dispel the myths surrounding the Indian and, in fact, in many instances they have perpetuated stereotypes.

Presently, there is a lot of discussion going on about building self-esteem among Native students. Very little has been said, and still less done, on how to develop respect and understanding *about* Native people among non-Natives. In other words, the majority of Canadians are excluded from educative exposure concerning Native people. This is a serious matter when one recognizes the fact that the prevailing attitudes of the dominant society affect, positively or negatively, the self-image of a minority group.

What better or faster medium is there than the school to display genuine appreciation of the Indian heritage? It is in school that the larger world begins to take on some meaning for most children. It is in school where negative attitudes towards Native people (which do not arise solely out of the school experience) can be redirected. Since a people cannot exist on an island, it is not enough for Native people to feel good about themselves; it is just as important that others share this feeling with them. Authentic, consistent exposure of the past and present of the Indian and Métis in the provincial curriculums of this country would contribute greatly towards bridging the startling, emotional separation between Native and non-Native Canadians.

One way to redirect the attitudes of white and Native persons towards each other is to include Native content as a significant, integral part of the provincial curriculums. Beyond this, the Indian heritage has a lot to offer to the Canadian society. There are many

Although the teacher in this particular Cree Kindergarten may well present students with a well-rounded perspective of Indians past and present, all too often teachers and children alike find it difficult to discuss Native people in anything but the past tense.

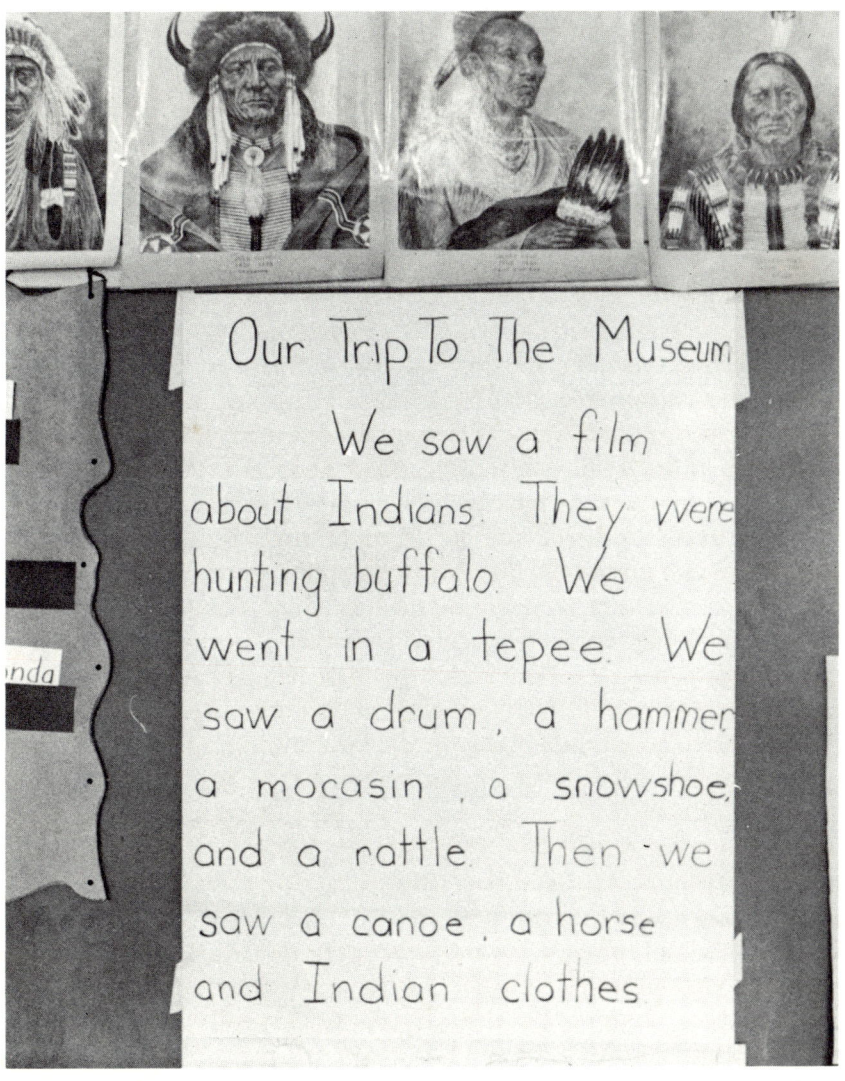

reasons why Canadian schools can no longer delete Indian and Métis history. To name a few: North American history begins with Native peoples, not Columbus; the great explorers of Canada were really the numerous (and nameless) Native peoples; the Indian and Métis people expended their time, energy, resources, and sometimes even their lives towards the settling and building of Canada; much has yet to be learned from the theology/philosophy/*Weltanschauung* of the Indian people and subsequently their value systems, which have contemporary relevance to our troubled society; and history which is truthful to the Native experience has yet to be learned.

Indian and Métis contributions to Canada have never been duly recognized. This handbook, then, is written, not so much to "help Natives" as it is to elevate Native heritage to its rightful place in Canadian society which would enrich all of us. It is written, in part, to remind educators and students of this fact. Hopefully, the handbook will act as a catalyst towards this end.

However, the handbook is written primarily to raise questions and issues for those who are in the process of teaching, or considering teaching, Native Studies. It is addressed not only to those who teach Native students, but to all educators who teach *about* Native people.

Amidst the fervor and frenzy of Intercultural Education and/or Native Studies programs, it is easy to ask the wrong questions, or to give answers before there are questions. In the same context, there is the danger of perpetuating existing myths about the subject being taught. For example, many teachers in their haste to teach Native culture equate this culture with external and ancient artifacts and thus present a stultified picture of the Indian. Hopefully, the handbook raises issues which will activate us to move beyond this frozen image.

The material is neither original nor comprehensive. It is only a beginning reminder of all there is to learn from the Indian heritage. It is at least a recognition on the part of all those who participated in this project of the need for much deeper involvement in the area.

Personal statement

This handbook is in no way a political or a definitive representation of Native people. While the author draws upon her experiences as a Native (who has worked for Native organizations), it is to be fully recognized that the issues and questions she raises, and the stereotypes she exposes are from her own observations and her own research.

Although the handbook is sprinkled with pointers, suggested approaches and hints, and although specific materials are recommended at the end of the text, it focuses on being essentially general. The author feels that one cannot do justice to a specific curriculum in so short a text, and, furthermore, no one person can be a final authority on Native people, or any other people for that matter.

Having made these cautioning remarks, the author sincerely hopes that readers enjoy the contents. More than that, she hopes readers will learn, even as she learned while writing it.

2
Heritage or Culture?

A few years ago, a friend and I were watching color television in a modern high-rise apartment. Like thousands of other Canadians, we were enjoying the Stanley Cup Playoffs. Suddenly my friend burst out, "I don't know anything about my culture! I am supposed to be an Indian working for a Native organization, but I don't know anything about my culture."

On many occasions the concern my friend raised had been my concern, too; a concern which causes an inner struggle shared by most contemporary Indians. But just then it struck me that perhaps the high-rise, the television and hockey were our culture, too. This was our present life-style; so then, was it not our culture? Perhaps we needed to rephrase the question. Obviously, we were living our *culture*; it was our *heritage* we knew so little about.

One of the most severe problems the Native person is faced with today is that he is defined outside himself. That is, other cultures and other people have defined who he is supposed to be as well as what he was supposed to have been. He has been defined, categorized and mythologized by books, movies, missionaries, educators, anthropologists—and every other "-ologist". He has been set apart by legality and even by economic status.[1] And within most of these existing categorizations of Indianness is a disturbing confusion between the past and present, or between heritage and culture.

Let me give you an example of how this confusion works and how it spreads. Recently, I had the task of speaking to a class of Grade 3 students in an Edmonton school. The teacher asked for what she called a "contemporary" Indian. She asked that the speaker emphasize the Indians of today.

When the children entered the classroom they brought with them a painted cardboard model resembling a totem pole which they placed beside me. Out of curiosity I asked them to tell me all they knew about the Indians of today. Without much hesitation they gave the following information: that Indians live in teepees, other Canadians live in houses; Indians use bows and arrows for hunting, others have guns; Indians use horses for transportation, others have cars; Indians use buffalo for food and clothing, others do not; and that Indians wear feathers.

"What is Indianness based on anyway? Is one an Indian because of race, a certain life-style, a religion, a geographical location or a language? Or even a treaty number?"

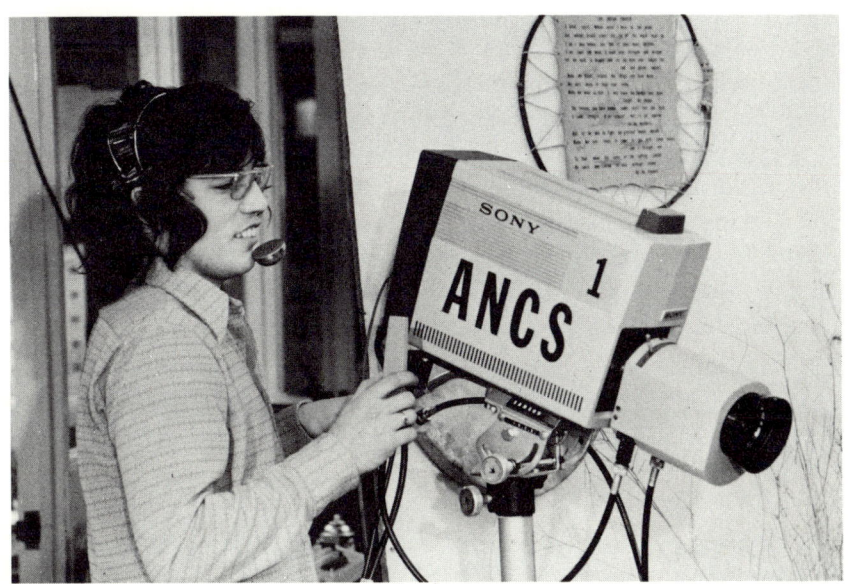

I asked if they knew that these traits reflected the past more than the present. Some answered in the affirmative, but in the same breath asked me to do a rain dance! They also wanted me to show them how to make a totem pole and a canoe and how "to speak Indian".

It was incredibly difficult for these children to distinguish the present from the past. The teacher knew this and was struggling with the issue. She herself realized that Indians of today do not live as described by the children, if they ever did, but she said there was very little material available on the contemporary Native peoples.

This I believe is a widespread phenomenon in our schools. Consequently, whenever we ask children what they think of Indians, or who they think Indians are, they invariably recall the Hollywood image of them. Even many Native children are similarly confused.

The Native people express the dilemma with specific questions. A northern student may wonder if he has to remain in the bush to maintain his Indianness. Those who chose an urban existence wonder quietly if they have not become "Uncle Toms"—a term no one understands. At one time or another perhaps we all ask ourselves, "Who is an Indian?" What is Indianness based on anyway? Is one an Indian because of race, a certain life-style, a religion, a geographical location or a language? Or even a treaty number?

A few decades ago some Native individuals began to venture out from their reserves or Métis communities. Most of them came back to stay and many came back with vehicles, phonographs or other unfamiliar gadgets. These individuals were often greeted with "Eh-queh-moo-neyakasoochik" by their people. The word means "They are pretentiously trying to be white". In a similar vein, recent revolutionary rhetoric (aided by saccharine liberals) reverts to the term "Uncle Tom" which essentially says the same thing as "Eh-queh-moo-neyakasoochik", except that "Uncle Tom" refers to any minority.

These accusations could be shrugged off if it were not for the fact that most ordinary citizens also think this way. That is, whenever Native peoples attempt to join the mainstream of Canadian society it is almost assumed that they are indeed trying to be white. In fact, it is often assumed (especially in university discussions) that Native people are faced with only two choices: to remain Indian (synonymously associated with staying on reserves or in the bush) and eventually perish, or to join society, which is erroneously linked with becoming white. And, unfortunately, many Native people still believe that if they make any gestures towards comfortable survival, they are trying to be white.

This belief that there are only two choices left for Native people further reflects a mix-up between heritage and culture. It is treating Indian history as if it were frozen at a fixed point in time; as if Indians cannot change and adapt with the rest of humanity. It is not taking into account the fact that considerable change has and is occurring in all peoples, and certainly in Indians.

Besides, whoever thought of accusing the first European settlers of trying to become Indian when they arrived on Indian land and were fed and taught survival skills by Indians? How about the missionaries who learned the Indian languages? Did anyone call them Indian? Did a Scot become a non-Scot when he no longer wore his kilt or played the bagpipes? Furthermore, a Ukrainian, a Frenchman or an East Indian is allowed to remain a Ukrainian, a Frenchman, and so forth even when he is a Canadian national. Then why is it so difficult to acknowledge that an Indian can remain Indian in any society? Why is he singled out from the possibility of change? Or why is there a stigma attached when he does change?

To be sure, many answers can be given to the above questions and some will be alluded to in the following pages. However, perhaps one of the underlying reasons why there is such confusion between heritage and culture is the failure to distinguish between traditional values and existing values. This is especially evident when educators mention "Indian culture" and then proceed to speak in terms of the past.

There is yet another angle to this discussion on heritage and culture. It is complicated because it revolves around the meaning of culture. It is not my purpose to get into an academic debate; I simply want to point out that "Indian culture" is so often equated with external trappings such as moccasins, beadwork, powwows, and of course, the feathers. To be sure, these things were, and in some cases still are representative of the Indian (at least the Plains Indian). But this

" ... even though the Indian has been faithful to his ancient values he has become, 'Not fossilized, unadaptive, not sealed into the past, but plastic, adaptive, assimilative ... ' "

view has neglected and fails to appreciate Native values and the thinking that is eventually expressed in rituals, foods and mannerisms. Although outward manifestations are an integral part of the total way of life in any given culture, a lopsided emphasis on "externals" can only lead to a superficial understanding. In fact, it indicates just that.

Needless to say, most educators have been highly selective in their discussions of "Indian culture". The very process of selecting visible (and invariably artifactual) material as the totality of Indian culture breeds a two-fold confusion. Not only is the distinction between heritage and culture clouded; so is the projected image of the Native people. Hence, not only is there a need to separate the past from the present, there is also a need to present a wholistic picture of the Indian, whether he is being discussed in terms of the past or the present. In other words, if a teacher is discussing powwows, he should not only differentiate between the powwows of the 1800's and those of the 1970's, but he should also have some appreciation of the Indian world-view as expressed in his dancing.

If there is anything we need to keep in mind from our discussion on heritage or culture, it is the fact of change among the Native people. It is not a new fact; in 1947, John Collier noted in his great book, *Indians of the Americas*, that even though the Indian has been faithful to his ancient values he has become, "Not fossilized, unadaptive, not sealed into the past, but plastic, adaptive, assimilative ..."[2]

In the Context of the Classroom:

Native people must define themselves

That Native people have been defined by others is not only unfair, but also annoying to them. The responsible thing for educators to do now is to open their policies and their classrooms to Native people who are defining themselves, and there are encouraging indications that more educators are accepting this responsibility.

Native people are in the painful process of developing their identity. They are experiencing new emotions, gaining new insights and facing new challenges as their self-awareness grows in the context of a "post-everything" society. In terms of these new feelings, they are busy mapping out their future.

It is of utmost importance, then, to utilize Native thinking and Native talent whenever Natives are being discussed in classrooms.

It would be best to begin at home—that is, to invite local Native people. Ask them what their perceptions are concerning their past, present, and future. How do they view themselves *and* Canadian society? Together, think of ways to investigate meaningful interaction between whites and Natives in your community.

The point is, it seems senseless to go on discussing Indians—their "culture" and inevitably their "problems"—from a distance. It makes much more sense to learn from the people themselves.

Beyond people there are books, poems, and works of music and art created by the Native people. These things should also be used as resource materials.

Educators must not confuse present Indian culture with heritage

Teachers (and administrative policies) must grapple with the fact of change among Native peoples. This is no easy task because the remnants of the past thread their way into the present; this is only a natural consequence of change. However, if we hope to gain perspective on Native Studies, it is imperative that we differentiate between heritage and culture.

It is probably safe to begin by separating the past from the present; that is, simply begin where Native peoples are today. What are their present life-styles? Customs? Occupations? Religions? Their creative expressions? And what are the issues that concern them?

The following comments are general pointers related to the *presentness* of the Native scene:

1. Vocations

Native peoples live all across Canada, and represent about ten linguistic groups. Occupational interests more or less depend upon geographical locations. Many northern Natives are hunters, trappers or labourers. Southern Indians work at such things as agriculture, ranching and business. And of course, there is a growing number of Native youth who are entering universities and colleges. There are also artists, musicians, dancers, poets, writers, and so on.

2. Treaties

There are the treaties, which involve several issues. There is the question of how to interpret treaties into modern contexts. This is a responsibility and a challenge that faces all Canadians today. Along with this is the concept of aboriginal rights which deserves much more attention than it has received. Incidentally, a discussion of aboriginal rights will probably lead into a discussion of colonialism, which could lead into a discussion of differing world-views, systems and cultures. Also, comparisons could be made with other treaties signed elsewhere between other indigenous peoples and colonial powers.[3]

But back to treaties, which of course leads us to The Indian Act. The Indian Act is very important to treaty Indians. Why? And how do the courts view it?

The outcome of the Lavell case is some indication of the legal viability of the Indian Act. Briefly, the Lavell case* involved Jeannette Corbierre (now Lavell) who, after marrying a white man, lost her rights and status as an Indian. The Indian Act is based on a patriarchal system: an Indian male retains his Indian status no matter whom he marries (in fact, the woman becomes legally Indian even if she is not an Indian by birth, while an Indian woman loses her legal status and rights when she marries a non-Indian). Feeling that such a disinheritance is in direct conflict with the Canadian Human Rights Bill, Mrs. Lavell appealed to the courts. The legal strength of the Indian

---

* Jeanette Lavell's case was tried in August, 1971 and the hearing before the Supreme Court of Canada took place in February, 1973. In August, 1973 the ruling came down with a 4 - 5 decision against Mrs. Lavell.

The Lavell case. "The legal strength of the Indian Act was tested in the Supreme Court of Canada and the Indian Act won. Or did it?"

Act was tested in the Supreme Court of Canada—and the Indian Act won.

Or did it? What are the implications behind the court's decision? For Indians? For women? For the Human Rights Bill, hence for all Canadians? Is the patriarchal system consistent with Indian traditions? What was the status of Indian women in the past? (Undoubtedly, it varied from tribe to tribe.) What is the status of Indian women today?

3. Non-treaty Natives

Then there are those Native* people who are not treaty Indians. As a matter of fact, the majority of Native Canadians have no treaty relationship with the Canadian government. They are often referred to as non-status Indians or Métis. Some may be full-blooded Indians who have not signed any treaties, or who have opted out of the treaties, but the majority are the Métis or Halfbreed people. They are perhaps the most neglected, and the least understood people in Canadian history. Although the Métis and the Indians are lumped together in most Native Studies curriculums, their histories and their cultures, and even their current concerns are different, even if their social problems are often quite similar.

The Halfbreed history in North America probably began a few months after the arrival of the white man. In Canada, the Métis formed a viable culture and community especially in the Red River area of what is now Manitoba. They very effectively adapted to both the Indian and white cultures, and were often bilingual. To date, they have not been duly recognized for the crucial role they played in bridging cultural and language barriers between the whites and the Indians. Nor have they been recognized for their contributions in transportation, especially from around 1840 to 1870, when they were strategically located in the heart of the continent.[4]

Perhaps because there is little sympathetic material available on Louis Riel, he is often studied as an incidental and incendiary personality in Canadian history. His enigmatic image is so played-up that

---

* The term "Native" as used here refers to both Indians and Halfbreeds (Métis), because both are of aboriginal descent.

his people and their concerns then (and now) have been largely forgotten. The hysteria caused by the death of the young and impetulant Thomas Scott under Riel's provisional government, and later the chaotic Frog Lake "massacre", has apparently distracted most historians from depth and objectivity in their reporting.

In any case, after the insurrection in Manitoba when many Métis were uprooted from their land and livelihood, they moved west—and many are still very mobile. When the promised *scrips* for land did not come, or were too slow in coming after the so-called second Riel Rebellion of 1885, many Métis became *squatters* on Crown land.[5] There were no treaties signed. Currently, the biggest difference between Indians and Métis is the legal difference; however, in some instances, there is also a vast cultural difference.

While many treaty Indians live on the 42 reservations of Alberta, for instance, the province's 60,000 Métis and non-status Indians do not... although, some live on the fringes of the reserves because their relatives may be treaty Indians. However, most Métis in Alberta live in communities of their own, or in the eight Métis Colonies that exist in the province. Many Alberta Métis, especially the older generation, speak a Native language and are culturally aligned with Indians. Their social and economic problems include health, housing, education, employment, discrimination and alcohol.

This situation reflects the national scene: the population of Indians in Canada is approximately 300,000. Of these only about 155,000 live on reserves, the rest are on Crown land or scattered among the general population. The majority of the country's 200,000 Métis, as in Alberta, live in close contact with reserve Indians in neighboring communities or in fringe settlements around the larger population centers.

4. Poverty

It seems that any discussion on the contemporary Native unavoidably leads to the topic of poverty. In a later chapter I elaborate on poverty, but for now let me just say that an obsession with this topic so often obscures other related and equally important realities. Namely, that in the last decade Native people across Canada have made a concerted effort to solve their problems, and as a result, many positive changes have and are taking place in Native communities.

While it may be realistic to lay bare the facts of poverty, it is equally important that students know that not all Native people are sitting on their haunches expecting others to solve things for them.

The other point to note is that poverty does not belong solely to Indians. Several years ago in a sociology class on social problems, I recall wondering if anyone else was poor, because the professor repeatedly referred to Native people as statistical examples of poverty. Since then I have heard and read so much about the "plight of Indian people", that I almost feel guilty for not starving! In the minds of most Canadians, poverty and Indians are like Siamese twins. Recently, a well-known Edmonton journalist was chiding a revivalist preacher for neglecting to attend to social problems like "the Indians, the Métis, the mentally-retarded, and the handicapped". A few sentences later—as I was munching my way back to the refrigerator for my nth helping—I read that we Natives were also "impoverished".

Not for one moment would I make light of the ugly effects of poverty. But if classroom groups must talk about Indians and poverty, then they must also point out the ways in which Native people are operating on this cancer. To be sure, the operations are always struggles and sometimes failures, but each new operation is faced with more experience, more skill, more confidence and more success.

Native organizations are one of the tools used to combat problems. If teachers and students hope to keep up with current concerns, then knowledge of the existence and functions of Native organizations is important. It would also be useful and enlightening to study the evolution of Native movements. In Alberta some major organizations are:

> The Indian Association of Alberta
> The Métis Association of Alberta
> Alberta Native Communications Society
> The Alberta Indian Education Center
> The Voice of Alberta Native Women's Society
> Native Counseling Services of Alberta
> The Kainai News Media
> Canadian Native Friendship Centers
> Poundmaker's Lodge
> INSPOL (Indian Sports Olympics)
> Canative Housing

Friendship Centers across Canada such as this one are important tools developed by Native people to combat problems.

The Red Paper, a collective statement of Native grievances to the Federal government, is studied by members of the Federation of Saskatchewan Indians at Carleton University.

Organizations in other provinces include:

>The Manitoba Métis Federation
>The Manitoba Métis Federation News
>The Métis Society of Saskatchewan
>The Native Brotherhood of British Columbia
>National Association of Friendship Centers (Thunder Bay, Ontario)
>Canadian Association In Support of the Native Peoples (Toronto)
>Nishnawbe Institute (Toronto)

National groups include the National Indian Brotherhood (and its recent offspring, the Indian Political Party of Canada) and the Native Council of Canada, which concerns itself with Métis issues. And of course countless Native individuals are expending their time, energies and talents on behalf of their people. These include elders, politicians, speakers, authors, journalists, artists, musicians, poets, photographers, educators, various counsellors, and so on. Some work within organizations while others are on their own. Again, it is stressed that such individuals should be utilized in classrooms as sources of information, points of view, insights and interaction.

5. "Urban Dilemma"

The "urban dilemma" usually comes up in any discussion on poverty. Native people have moved, and are now even more rapidly moving, into cities and towns. It is true that so many come unprepared both economically and culturally. Not all have come voluntarily, a particular example being northern students who have to come to cities and towns to continue their education. Consequently, many Native people have been hurt, frustrated, disillusioned, and embittered.

There is nothing wrong with exposing the Indian's urban problems because, hopefully, it will heighten the sensitivities of the students and teachers. But again, there is a different side to the urban story. There are Native people who have very quickly and very comfortably adapted to traffic, noise, pollution, Chargex bills, gastritis, and other urban amenities.

More seriously, not all Natives fall flat on their faces the moment they hit town, as one could be led to believe by well-meaning journalists, and sometimes even by frustrated Native spokesmen. Not enough recognition or credit has been given to the hundreds of Natives who have found it psychologically and economically feasible to reside in cities. Many of these people have maintained ties with their non-urban friends and relatives, and continue to appreciate the values inherent in their heritage. These flexible people are, in most cases, adequately meeting the challenge of harmonizing the old with the new.

In conclusion, when one begins to appreciate the seemingly infinite possibilities of the facts, issues and problems involved in studying the contemporary Native, then one can imagine the scope and depth of his heritage. One can no longer teach about Indians and Métis in a simplistic, narrow or superficial manner. One cannot be content with a display of arrowheads, stuffed buffalo, papier-mâché tipis, CFRN* feather bonnets and cardboard totems.

Culture is more than a package of tangibles

A problem directly related to the confusion of the Native past and present is the misguided emphasis upon visible material. Undoubtedly, an exhibition of glistening quills, glossy beads, colorful feathers and beautiful Native costumes is appealing and exciting to children. One can certainly understand why teachers have been prone to teach "Indian culture" in such a limited fashion. But this selective treatment of "culture" negates a wealth of intangibles that are a vital and integral part of any culture. It is neither fair nor intellectually honest to fragment anyone's heritage or culture into unrecognizable bits and pieces. We must seek to be wholistic in our teaching.

For example, let's consider traditional Indian dancing. Several years ago it was a popular thing to invite "powwow" dancers and singers in their colorful costumes into classrooms. I had the opportunity to observe many of these activities. I noticed especially two things

---

* A local, Alberta radio station

in the students (whether elementary or secondary); their fascination with the feathered bustles and rhythm, and their inattention to explanations about the dances. While these onlookers often developed a fresh appreciation for the Indian's vivid sense of color and movement, they gained very little understanding of his values and thoughts.

Did they learn the functions of the drummer and singers? Were they aware that some dancers had special roles to play? Could they trace the origin of the dances? And most importantly, did they have any idea what the various dances meant? Could they list some of the new functions of contemporary "powwows"?

People involved in Native arts and crafts such as beadwork and moccasins often came along. Here again, students often learned little more than that Native women are capable of sewing with imagination. The students often missed out on the meaning of designs, color schemes, and choice of material.

This author highly encourages teachers to continue inviting Native dancers and folk artists into the classroom. However, teachers should seize these opportunities to deepen knowledge and appreciation for Native concepts and beliefs. The same idea applies to external displays. It is fine to expose students to tangible art, but it is equally important to point out what this art reflects. It is only through a well-rounded knowledge of each other's life-views and life-styles that different peoples can appreciate each other. In our goal to understand the inner life and spirit of a people, we must probe its art (as well as its religion, literature, poetry, music and dances) because it is one of the ways through which we express human perceptions and sensations.

1. Art

Indeed, studying Indian art in North America would be an excellent way to help students realize the vast differences that exist between Indian tribes. A comprehensive study would look at Indian art of at least eleven regions: Northwest Coast, California, the Basin Plateau, the Southwest, the Southern Plains, the Great Plains, the Canadian Plains, the Midwest, the Southeast, the Eastern Woodlands and the Eskimo. It would consider the evolution of Indian art from Pre-

Henry Nanooch, a contemporary Native Canadian artist

Columbian to modern times. Students would have the opportunity to research the influences of the white explorers, traders, missionaries, settlers and government. As an example, they could study the effects mission schools, such as French-Canadian convents for Indian girls, had upon the designs and styles in beadwork among the Eastern Woodland women. Then the students could move from the past to the present by studying contemporary Native Canadian artists such as Alberta's Gerald Tailfeathers, Alex Janvier, Henry Nanooch, and Sarain Stump, as well as those from other provinces including Arthur Shilling, Ross Woods, Ron Hamilton, Allen Sapp, Jackson Beardy, Daphne "Odjig" Beavon, Norval Morrisseau, Bob Davidson and Lloyd Caibaiosai.[6] And of course there are the countless (and so often the nameless) women whose diligent art work is sold in such places as Canadiana, Arctic Arts and the Hudson's Bay Company.

But beyond the value of learning that diversity as well as change exists among Indian peoples, an authentic examination of their art is perhaps the best channel through which we can understand their values and world-views.

Art has woven its way into so many facets of Indian life. Art objects were not only functional or simply aesthetic, but they were also at times expressions of the Indian's *Weltanschauung*. The Indian's inventive use of raw materials reflects his adaptive, rather than forceful, relationship to nature. His use of dolls, masks and costumes in ceremonies indicates his appreciation for artistic ritual, as well as his gestures to the gods. His abstract art probably symbolizes several things: such as his attempts to get at the essence of a thing (for example, to carve out the soul of a tree), or his attempts to express a relationship between human and non-human spirits. Perhaps much of his art derives from his dreams and visions. Or it may even derive from his humor, an outstanding trait which has received minimal recognition.

So many questions and value issues are involved when considering Indian art. In the first place, what is Indian art? Does it have consistent characteristics? How does one account for the high degree of regionalism? Since most art objects available are from the post-Columbian era, is there such a thing as "traditional" Indian art? For that matter, what is traditional art in any culture? If art is an expression of a people, and if people change, then what is the criteria for traditional art? Obviously, most art forms are a combination of the old and the new. How is this expressed in modern Indian art? Can a non-Indian do Indian art? Is art dependent upon racial origin?

Is art relative? Much of European art is based upon seven principles of organization: unity, variation, repetition, contrast, balance, movement, and climax. Should these seven principles be used as criteria when evaluating non-Western art? It has been said that beauty is in the eyes of the beholder. With this in mind, Indian art, then, like all art, should be examined within the context of its times and places. In other words, we should avoid judging Indian art ethnocentrically and/or anachronistically.

2. Religion

Art and religion often go hand in hand. Although the Indian tribes did not produce a systematic theology (in Western terms), most of them were deeply committed to certain attitudes, beliefs, and practises. In fact, many of the practises were rigidly institutionalized, and undoubtedly certain individuals adhered to their beliefs with as much ardor and faith as anyone else in any other religion has done. Religion is what ultimately brings meaning and makes sense out of life. The Indian artistically and often ritualistically expressed what made sense to him.

Alas, the white settlers and missionaries had little tolerance for Indian beliefs and their ways of expressing them (they assumed it was heathenism)—let alone any desire to understand them. The virtual absence of Indian religious studies from our universities and schools indicates just to what an extreme extent this lack of understanding has gone. Even in so many Native homes, there is little detailed knowledge of the religious part of their heritage.

But if there is any Indian renaissance today, it is in the world of religion. Young people are coming to the elders for spiritual guidance and the elders are once again sharing their secrets with them. Practises, such as the Sun Dance and the use of sweat lodges, which were once institutionalized but later prohibited by white laws, are coming back. The Indian's close communion with the earth is being

"In Alberta the popular Lac St. Anne pilgrimages reflect an inspiring combination of Indian traditions and Christianity."

recognized and re-affirmed, not only by himself, but also by others. His tribally-oriented life-style may be experiencing a rebirth. Vine Deloria Jr., who has written several books, is one of the more notable proponents of such a rebirth.[7]

Like art, religion is not static. Indians have indicated their knowledge of this fact with their historical willingness to listen to the Christian message, to select portions of it and to give other portions their own interpretations. The Native American Church has effectively mixed the two. In Alberta the popular Lac St. Anne pilgrimages reflect an inspiring combination of Indian traditions and Christianity.

It is incredible that after all these years, both Natives and non-Natives are just becoming aware of the scope and richness of Native religions. For various reasons Indian religions (hence, Indian values) have been clouded with mystery, and the problem remains (and perhaps it always will) in knowing the difference between prophets and charlatans. Furthermore, we can only speculate about what the Indian's traditional values were because the story of the Indian peoples was recorded almost entirely by those who neither spoke his language nor understood his ways. Still, we must rely on Native elders to share what they recall of the traditional beliefs. Also, the vestiges of the past still exist in varying degrees in most Native communities, and from them we can imaginatively retrace the origins of our values.

Summarily then, there is much more to the Native scene than buffalo, feathers, and the travois. It will not be easy to digress from the conventional path of teaching Indian "culture". However, in the interests of our multi-cultural, pluralistic ideals, we can at least begin to try.

3
Stereotypes: Past and Present

32 *Defeathering the Indian*

Defining culture in terms of heritage perpetuates stereotypes about the North American Indian. Indeed, it is a vicious circle, for the existing stereotypes, which came from the past, continue to point back to the past.

The various stereotyped images of Native people

Soon after Columbus accidentally "discovered" America, Indian peoples were depicted essentially under two categories, the noble red man and the savage.

The noble red man was the perfect primitive; the lithe, swarthy one who could walk through the driest twigs without making a noise. He was of a people "whose natures could hardly be told save through the language of music; peoples joyously hospitable who seemed as free as birds, whose speech and colors were like the warbling and plumage of birds".[1] No wonder people back in Europe, like Jean Jacques Rousseau, got excited about this unique specimen of Utopian man!

But alas, in North America, the romance soon ended between the "primitive native" and the aggressive white man. When the indigenous peoples finally began defending their very lives and their ways of life against the invaders; lo, they became savages overnight. This is borne out in history book after history book, where Indians are described as "ferocious", "warlike", "hostile" and, of course, "savage".*

It was the Indian of the white man's imagination rather than the Indian of historical fact who finally became dominant in English-American literature. This fact has had a long-range effect upon the Indian image; the myth of both the nobility and the savagery of the Native is not dead. It has been transported into modern times. Today many non-Natives still view the Indian in either of two ways, as a sublime "Nature-lover" or as a "Dirty Indian".

The Nature-lover is the resurrected noble red man. He is the inspired, sagacious aborigine, often referred to as the elder. He is

---

* Words are discussed further in a later section of this handbook, pp. 50-53.

usually silent in his wisdom, but whenever he opens his mouth a flow of profundities pours out. If he suffers, he suffers silently if not stoically. He communes with the spirits of the plains, streams, woods and hills. He is at peace with the world around him. He is the gray-haired poet. The gentle orator. The colorful dancer. He is the mellow-voiced spokesman of conservation and ecology.

On the other extreme is the Dirty Indian. He is the sinister shadow of the savage. He does not come to work on time; he does not even stick to his job. He is not dependable. He is irresponsible. He is lazy and his house is usually not clean. He is perpetually on welfare. And when he is drunk, he is usually sullen and hostile. Sometimes, however, he is outrageously loud and disturbs someone's peace—if not someone's lawn!

A more recent image (which is really just an extension of the savage Indian myth) is the militant Indian, the embodiment of Red Power. This is the bitter, angry Indian. He is the Indian who harangues the white man at every opportunity. He is the warrior risen from the dead and he is expected to explode in the very near future.

Now let's go back to some semblance of sanity. Although stereotypes usually have some elements of truth in them, they are almost always very destructive, and the immorality of stereotypes is this: they not only hide truth; they prevent it. And the stereotyping of Indian peoples is a good example of how this happens.

Undoubtedly, there were noble Indian people, just as surely as there were those who were capable of savagery. However, there was much, much more to Indian life than just being noble or being savage. But the persistence of these stereotypes has obscured the richness and variety inherent in Indian cultures.

Similarly the present perspectives of Native people as simply Nature-lovers, Dirty Indians and Red-Power militants prevents them from being seen for what they are—human beings.

1. The Myth of the Nature-lover

There is ample evidence that most Native peoples were and are lovers of nature. Indeed they lived, and many continue to live, openly with nature. Their basic world-view revolves around a oneness with the earth and its web of life. They accept themselves as one among many creatures in the physical universe; hence, their respect for human personality.

Still, romanticizing Native peoples as Nature-lovers is damaging because the image tends to be presented in a very superficial way. The philosophy that underlies the Indians' closeness with nature is usually circumvented. Perhaps a more serious outcome of this particular stereotype is that the Indian has been so closely associated with nature that sometimes he is hardly separated from it at all. Consider phrases like "young buck" or "feathered friends". Many authors have been guilty of comparing Indian virtues to animal characteristics. As an example, in a recent book, *Agouhanna*, the author described "the little Iroquois ... silent as fish in a stream ... "[2] Later on he writes, "Happy, they flexed their growing muscles like young animals".[3] In other cases, animals are not at all clearly distinguished from their Indian masters. In the book *Without Reserve*, Sheila Burnford describes a particular dog as, "part husky, part wolf, part Indian dog".[4]

It is good and well that in our classrooms Native peoples are credited as the original defenders of ecology, but again, they are more than this. This is especially true today when there are thousands of urbanized Native peoples.

2. The Myth of the Dirty Indian

Speaking of urbanization ... let's discuss the myth of the Indian as lazy, dirty and drunken. Of all the stereotypes about Natives, that is perhaps the most tragic. It has bred distrust, suspicion, bitterness and even hatred between contemporary whites and Indians. It has often blocked all communication between the two groups.

The myth of the Dirty Indian was likely reinforced when Native peoples began to migrate into cities and towns. Initially, cities and towns were strange and frightening places (and they still are for many Northern Natives). Many came with hopes of finding jobs or simply searching for new life-styles. Most were totally unprepared for what they found (or did not find, such as jobs). Disillusioned, and dazed with culture shock, if not future shock, many Native people had few alternatives but to resort to welfare.

A tree, powerless against the encroachments of the builder and developer, echoes the "feeling of lostness" experienced by many Northern Natives in their first encounters with cities and towns.

It must be said here that Native people came to the cities and towns when their traditional ways of life were either threatened or destroyed. And by leaving familiar surroundings, although it appeared to be a solution, they deepened their feeling of lostness. There is nothing intrinsically sacred about tradition, but its premature destruction often creates a social vacuum. The self-sufficiency of a people is often destroyed in this process. Lost as well are traditional outlets for self-expression and self-actualization which are necessary for a people to have positive self-concepts.

In Canada, Indian cultures were permanently altered when the buffalo was systematically annihilated.[5] Because the Indians could not accept the cow as a replacement for the buffalo (the buffalo was the basis of the biggest single tradition among the Plains Indians), a social vacuum was ultimately created. Disease, starvation, the missionaries, the police, and the whiskey traders compounded the problems. The death of a livelihood is the death of self-sufficiency.

It has been a century since the destruction of the buffalo, but what a domino effect has occurred because of it! The death of the buffalo (or beaver or moose or caribou) still reverberates in welfare offices and/or bar rooms. Despite the global idolization of modern technology, Native people have not found it a sufficient enough tradition to adequately fill the vacuum that the destroyed animals have left.

In any case being poor and having difficulties with alcohol (the two are inextricably related) has made many Native people highly visible in Canadian society. Hence, the Dirty Indian.

3. The Social Problem

At the outset, let me say that Native people *do* have problems. There are Native *individuals* who are dirty, unreliable, irresponsible, on welfare, and perpetually drunk. Also, there is a kernel of truth in the Dirty Indian image. But, again, this obscures at least two things that should be obvious: that the majority of Native people are not unclean, unreliable and lazy, and that being non-Native does not remove the possibility of such characteristics. In the area of alcohol, the fact that alcohol is probably the number one struggle, if not the number one killer among Native people, should not lessen the reality that alcohol is a *universal* problem.

Perhaps a more important point to make is that the concepts of cleanliness, responsibility and work are viewed differently by both groups.

In the matter of cleanliness, let me give you an example. Several summers ago when I was intern-teaching in a northern reserve, one of the teachers told me how she "had to get used to" the smells of the children. She insisted it was not just stuffiness, but a "peculiar odor".

It was a beautiful summer, a summer northern Natives enjoy. There were fishes to be caught and smoked. There was moosehide to be tanned, and as always pesky mosquitoes to be repelled with smudge. Oddly enough, the "peculiar" smell was a redolent mixture of spruce, moosehide, and woodsmoke. All the while this teacher was complaining about the smell of the children, the children were reporting about a "strange" odor within the vicinity of some of the teachers. It was the ammonia used by some of the teachers for their chemical toilets. And it never seemed to occur to the teacher that she could be giving off odors.

More to the point, both the teacher and the children attached value judgements to unfamiliar odors. As a friend of mine noted, "To a person whose culture evidently prefers Chanel No. 5 or pine-scented aerosol cans, moosehide and woodsmoke can seem foreign". The converse is also true, I might add.

Responsibility is also judged according to cultural priorities. A white, middle-class man is judged responsible when he chooses a career which is economically secure, and still more so if it is socially prestigious as well. Along with this he is expected to bind his marriage and children (in that order!) by legality. Once he settles comfortably into his career and home life, he will be responsible for the future of his wife and children; he will invest. Our banks and our national economy thrive on the concept of saving for the future.

Traditionally, the Indian concept of responsibility was not based on climbing the social ladder. Responsibility meant, and still does in the communities that are yet intact, contributing to the welfare of the

group—the family, clan or tribe. Even today in northern areas, a young man may quit school or leave a stable job so that he can help out his aging father or uncle on the trapline. Such a young man would be considered highly irresponsible by one set of standards; yet very responsible by another. This dilemma should help us understand why many Native young people have been so bewildered. Whose standards should they follow?

Work is a relative concept also. It can be an "activity in which one exerts strength or faculties to do or perform something" (*Webster's Dictionary*), or it can be an attitude, a world-view. Europeans came to the American continent entrenched in what has become known as the work ethic. Indeed, it was probably because of the work ethic that they came.

A brief discourse on the work ethic as a world-view is of necessity superficial and simplistic. Nonetheless, one of the more succinct descriptions of it is in the following quotation: "In our world a man's worth is determined by his work. The aim of life—whether you are conservative or liberal, young or old, Christian or non-Christian—is to keep the wheels moving in order to earn more money in order to raise your standard of living in order to get another car in order to ..."[6]

Generally speaking, the work ethic revolves around "progress", "getting ahead", "making life better", or "stepping up". To one who does not grow up with such views towards life, the work ethic appears to be an attitude of being compulsively dissatisfied.

A misunderstanding between white settlers and Indian peoples was inevitable because the aim of life for the Indians was not work. As previously discussed, the Indian's world-view revolved around the earth and his relationship with his society. However, in terms of physical exertion the Indians certainly had their share of work. Hunting, trapping, fishing, farming, and trekking through rivers and mountains for white explorers can hardly be considered play.

One is not necessarily lazy because one does not subscribe to the work ethic. One's industriousness is not necessarily determined by the work one does. Conversely, one can certainly be lazy within the work ethic.

Indians may have appeared lazy to the settlers because they were not doing what was defined as work by the settlers; that is, chopping down trees and tearing up land. Unfortunately, there are still many non-Natives who judge Native people as lazy, and the judgement is still often based on distant and superficial glances at Native people.

Unravelling the myth of the Dirty Indian entails a study of the sociological definition of a "problem" because the myth is fed on the assumption that the Indian is a "problem". I will not go into sociological semantics, but in terms of Indian—White relationships, at least two considerations emerge which tell us something about the concept of a social problem. One is that the dominant group assumes certain values are important and when a minority group fails to accept these assumptions, in word and in deed, the majority classifies the minority as an enigma. Hence, English Canada refers to the "French problem", the "Hutterite situation", and, of course, the "Indian problem". This thought leads to the second, which is that a social problem can only be defined in *relative* terms.

4. The Manifest Destiny

History tells us that it is not safe to be defined as a social problem by a dominant party (dominant in numbers and/or weapons) because the dominant group will eventually find "solutions" to the "problem". Seeing Native peoples as problems is as old as the doctrine of Manifest Destiny—a doctrine based on an incredible assertion that "The rich and beautiful valleys of Wyoming are destined for the occupancy and sustenance of the Anglo-Saxon race... The same inscrutable Arbiter that decreed the downfall of Rome has pronounced the doom of extinction upon the red men of America".[7] Once the new Americans assumed that the American continent was God's gift to them, the indigenous peoples remained only obstacles to be removed and the fact that these people were humans was scarcely acknowledged.

Nor can Canadians say that this approach was taken only in the United States. French and English settlers in Newfoundland established a direct and deliberate policy of extermination against the Beothuk Indians. They armed the Micmacs with firelock guns and offered a reward for every Beothuk scalp brought in, and the settlers viewed hunting the Beothuk as a form of blood sport, providing entertainment on a quiet Sunday. This slaughter continued for two and one-half centuries and resulted in the total extinction of the Beothuk nation.

Stereotyping is dangerous because of what it can do (and it has done so in the past) to otherwise decent human beings. Arrogant value assumptions compounded with untruths have been breeding grounds for Holy Crusades, forms of imperialism such as the Manifest Destiny doctrine, Hitlers, and Vietnams. The continuation of arrogant value assumptions is evident in the modern social service mentality.*

5. Stereotypes and Education

Analyzing stereotypes can be a tedious and certainly a delicate business. Understandably, educators may wonder how the above discussion relates to their administration or classroom headaches. But it does relate to the very business of an educator, which presumably includes the search for truth and loyalty to truth once it has been found. Nonetheless, educators are not exempt from human fallibility, and even they are vulnerable to gross generalizations, out of which come biased attitudes (or vice-versa). And biased attitudes are eventually reflected in administrative policies and in classrooms, both of which touch the lives of children.

Let me briefly illustrate with a personal story. My earliest impressions of my elementary teachers were that they seemed surprised at my good grades, especially in spelling and reading. (I won't mention arithmetic.) My first teacher was so delighted at my ability to read through the Red, Yellow and Blue books on my first day of class that he forgot to tell me about pausing for commas and periods. I will never forget the disbelief on my next teacher's face when she asked me to read. I was in Grade 4—and still breathlessly roaring away at top speed, quite oblivious of punctuation!

Some not-so-amusing things happened inside me in Grades 5 and 6. I was attending a much larger school with many more white

---

* Further comments on value assumptions appear in the sections on jargon and compensatory education, pp. 54-59.

Indians demonstrate against administrative policies in education touching the lives of Native children.

children. Teachers seemed so cold and distant. They frightened me. Retrospectively, I think it was their attitude of resignation towards me that I could not understand. They were resigned to the belief that I, as a Métis child, was destined to fail. And how was I to appreciate such a low expectation? I could not know then that I was already marked as a Social Problem.

Grades 7 through 9, in a new location, were refreshing and different. I had the same teacher for all three grades. This teacher was consistently humane, sensitive and attentive. Reaching Grade 10 was no problem until I faced registration day at a very fundamentalistic, private high school. The principal called me to his office and flatly stated that I should enroll in a course leading to "secretarial opportunities" rather than to university. When I asked why, he meandered through several vague statements about my "background". Then when I asked what that had to do with "secretarial opportunities", he blandly asked, "You are Indian? Aren't you a bit slow?" I heard no more. As they say, "Curiosity killed the cat!" He also needlessly insulted secretaries.

The public in general has low expectations of Native people. Recently, on a train to Winnipeg, a woman beside me began discussing the "Indian problem". She listed the usual vices: "They're always drunk, they don't work and they're all on welfare". But she also said something—not once but several times—that caught my attention, "It's no use; we've tried everything. Nothing works for the Indian. It's no use—nothing will ever work". The tragedy is that so many Native people have also come to believe in the "failure-of-Indians" syndrome.

6. Human Beings—No More, No Less

If Native people are more than conservationists or social enigmas, then what are they? Needless to say, they are human beings—no more and no less. The ultimate ugliness of stereotyping is that it bypasses humanity. Neither the noble red man nor the savage Indian myth says much about Indians as human beings, people who are capable of "the good, the bad and the ugly". People who can laugh, cry, hate and love. People who have dreams, aspirations and hopes. People, like the rest of humanity, who are facing *and* adapting to change.

"What do Indians want?" is a question we often hear. Again, with the rest of humanity, Native people are concerned with the mundane but basic things of life: food, shelter, clothing and love. They are worried about inflation, the effects of alcohol, car accidents, health, and their children. As individuals, they are interested in relationships, in personal achievements and a myriad of other details. Native people are ordinary human beings with ordinary human wants. But Native people do not want to sacrifice their Indianness, their unique heritage, in order to have the basic necessities of life. And Native people feel that there is nothing inordinate about this simple desire, with which, ideally, Canadians would agree; that basic survival and personal freedom should not be diametrically opposed to each other.

In the Context of the Classroom:

Preparing lessons on stereotyping

Although the subject of stereotypes can come up on many occasions (for example during discussions on poverty, the urban dilemma, and the historical treatment of Native peoples in books, in Indian art and religion), it is very important that lessons be prepared on stereotyping itself. This should be done not only for the sake of the Native people, but for the benefit of everyone. Stereotyping is a universal phenomenon and it would not hurt to openly and intelligently discuss it all the way from kindergarten to university.

It is not enough for people to know that prejudice, discrimination and stereotypes exist. It is worthwhile to know the following:

    a. The nature of prejudice. What is it?
    b. How is prejudice acquired? What role can parents and teachers play in facilitating or preventing the development of prejudices?

Personal achievement . . . an ordinary human need

c. The meaning of discrimination. Discrimination is an action that results from an attitude of mind. What sort of actions are discriminatory? What is the difference between blatant and subtle discrimination?
d. Why are people prejudiced? Are they misinformed? Insecure? Is it because they need a scapegoat? Do they feel so inferior that they have to run down someone else? Do they simply feel racially superior?
e. The effects of prejudice. What happens to the victims? How do they feel—and how do they respond?
f. Group stereotypes. Almost every ethnic group is stereotyped to various degrees. What are these stereotypes? Why were they formed? How truthful are stereotypes? What role does history, and the various media play in perpetuating stereotypes?
g. How to tackle prejudice. We are all influenced by prejudicial feelings, so how can we objectively deal with them? Perhaps a combination of self-knowledge, awareness of history and of one's society, and sensitivity to all human beings would help.
h. What can a community do to fight discrimination? Perhaps it would involve information seminars and even legal action.
i. What can classrooms do to combat prejudice, discrimination and stereotypes? How significant is it to choose books, films, study guides and illustrations with care and awareness?

Preparing lessons on how cultures clash

Closely related but somewhat different is the question of how cultures clash.

a. And when do cultures clash? What role does ethnocentricity play?
b. Compare different world-views and value systems.
c. Why do cultures impose their systems on others? As an example, why does America feel that world peace is dependent upon her existence?
d. Is it possible for differing world-views to live side by side?

e. Is a "global village" the answer? Then who would determine the standards in this village?
f. We are faced with the task of surviving. How long can we survive with hate, violence and war?
g. What can we do to alter our seeming addiction to destruction? How can we become peacemakers?

Perhaps we could all benefit from a course on Peace Studies where we would search for ways to live peaceably as neighbors, despite differing cultures and international barriers.

4
The Media and The Indian

The printed word, language, and pictures

1. History Books

Most educated people today are aware that most history books described Indians as savage, ferocious, wild, uncivilized, primitive, barbaric, fierce, pagan, hostile, warlike, *et. al., ad nauseum*. These people would agree that the above words have been harmful to the Indian image, and would refrain from using them, and some even courteously mumble an apology when they slip out a word like "primitive".

However, many of these very same people often treat these historical documents on Indians as gospel truth. This uncritical acceptance of history books negates two very crucial points—not only were those descriptions based on blatant ethnocentricity, which makes them suspect; but also twentieth-century western standards are used to assess sixteenth-century Indian life.

a. Ethnocentricity

First, let's elaborate on ethnocentricity, which Webster defines as "regarding one's own race or cultural group as superior to others". Prejudice, which literally means "judging in advance", and ethnocentricity are interrelated. When one considers himself superior, he mechanically judges others to be inferior. And just to make sure he is superior, he creates characteristics in others to confirm their inferiority, using his standards as criteria, of course.

Perhaps no clearer example of "judging in advance" can be found than in the use of the term "savage" and all its synonyms. The height of ethnocentricity is to call someone else barbarian . . . primitive or uncivilized. It is to set oneself up as a measuring stick of civilization. Furthermore, it is to assume that one is exempt from barbarity and savagery. So the explorers, while they were being fed, guided and otherwise aided by the Indians, either killed and tortured them or insulted them in their writings. Hernando de Soto, Spanish explorer of the southeastern United States, was one of the more notorious examples of civilized behaviour: "Again and again, having been received with hospitality, he kidnapped the headmen or chiefs. He burned the villages, laid waste the cornfields, dragged Indians with

The present and the past co-exist in the culture of contemporary Indians: a mobile home industry on the Blackfoot Reserve at Standoff, Alberta, points the way to future self-sufficiency; while passing of the traditional peace pipe on Treaty Day evokes memories of the past.

him from place to place in chains as carriers, and applied torture to extract information. These are not stories told by the Indians. They come from ... de Soto's companion and eulogist, the Gentleman of Elvas".[1] And this Gentleman of Elvas, despite all the atrocities he had witnessed eulogized de Soto as " ... the magnanimous, the virtuous, the intrepid captain ... "[2]

Jacques Cartier behaved similarly in Canada. In 1535 he landed at Stadacona and spent the winter there. At one point all but three of his men were seriously ill with scurvy and probably they all would have died if it hadn't been for a remedy made from the boughs of evergreen trees which the Indians showed them how to make. After receiving this kindness and many other forms of hospitality from the Indians, Cartier reciprocated by kidnapping several of them for exhibit in Europe.

There were missionaries who wrote off the Indian as wild pagans. Blessed, supported and encouraged by government and military agencies, many missionaries in their sincere attempts to save Indian individuals (apparently only for the after-life) at the same time worked hard to destroy Indian societies. As part of the scheme to chisel away Indian paganism, the men's cherished locks and braids were sheared for church services; at which time the missionaries proudly presented to the astonished Indians pictures of their blond saviour in shoulder-length hair!

Perhaps the most vicious accounts of Indian people were written in the 1880's. It was a violent era in which the Plains Indians finally vigorously resisted white invasion after having witnessed several centuries of broken promises and violence done to them. Settlers and soldiers were quick to use this resistance as a confirmation that the Indian was indeed fierce, hostile and warlike; ever "lurking" just outside stockades, and ever ready to pounce upon defenseless women and children and always accompanied by his blood-curdling war-whoop.

When Indians employed scalping, white people were horrified, apparently forgetting that scalping was considered rather virtuous by the English in 1755 when they set bounties on the Penobscot Indian scalps.[3]

Most history books have been quick to note that, despite his desperate ferocity, the Indian lost. What these history books often failed to mention was that, not only did the Indian fight in self-defense, and often in revenge, but that there was desperate ferocity on both sides. Consider Lieutenant James Conner's description of the Sand Creek massacre by Colonel Chivington: "In going over the battleground the next day I did not see a body of man, woman, or child but was scalped, and in many instances their bodies mutilated in the most horrible manner—men, women, and children's privates cut out, etc.; I heard one man say that he had cut out a woman's private parts and had them for exhibition on a stick; I heard another man say that he had cut the fingers off an Indian to get the rings on the hand; according to the best of my knowledge and belief these atrocities that were committed were with the knowledge of J.M. Chivington, and I do not know of his taking any measures to prevent them; . . . "[4]

The point to be made is that historians, in their haste to record Indian attacks on wagon trains, stage lines and military outposts, neglected to list the deeds of Carleton, Carson, Chivington, Connor, Sherman, Sheridan, Custer and Forsyth, just to mention a few. Most Canadian history books have failed to mention the Cypress Hills massacre of 1872, for instance, which took place in Alberta. Thirty Assiniboines were shot up by a motley crew of white men from what is now Montana (Fort Benton) on the pretense that they were tracking down horse thieves. Perhaps the historians had queasy stomachs. They certainly had an ingenious way of separating the wheat from the chaff; when the Indians attacked the whites it was a "massacre", but when the whites invaded the Indians it was simply a "fight".[5] When the Indians tried to save what was left of their life-styles, they were savages; when the soldiers indiscriminately wiped out village after Indian village, they were civilized. Indeed, the historian's sense of civilization boggles the mind.

Yet, it is this selective and ethnocentric viewpoint of civilization that has filtered into every classroom in North America. Hence, the myth of the Indian both as a warrior and as a savage has persisted right into our century.

b. Anachronisms

So often, Western norms of our century have been used to assess the quality of Indian life at least several hundred years removed. For example, the descriptions of the Indian's personal habits, descriptions based on times in which no one could brag of cleanliness, have been judged by the fastidious standards of today.

Another example is the horrified reaction to the seventeenth-century Indian's method of torturing his captives. It is well to disdain torture, but why should the eighteenth-century Puritan's method of executing witches be any less horrifying? And how can this napalm-using century possibly judge another era for torture?

Anachronisms exist in our North American history textbooks, partly because of the confusion between heritage and culture, and partly because textbooks persist in avoiding the contemporary Native.

So much more needs to be said about North American history books, and certainly more needs to be done—like rewriting most of them! At least one thing appears to favor all those who have been subject to discrimination in textbooks. (The author fully realizes that most people have been subject to discrimination, depending on who wrote the textbook). Within the last decade *obvious* prejudice has become much less respectable. However, one fears that blatancy has been replaced with subtlety. For example, take the concept of "compensatory education".

2. Jargon that Speaks

It seems that in the early 1960's it suddenly dawned on researchers and educators that there were reasons why some children, especially those from low economic groups, were failing and/or dropping out of school. After countless reports they discovered that children of low-income families were often lacking in "adequate living conditions, clothing, exercise, and the availability of medical care ... "[6] Then a profound conclusion was reached: "These deficiencies in basic needs operate to influence learning in a number of ways".[7] It was decided that this had some implications for the schools, and that "no child should be permitted or expected to learn under such adverse

"Does the school exist for the child, or is the child to conform to the set patterns and expectations of the school?"

circumstances as hunger, fatigue, disease, or impaired bodily functions".[8]

If educators had not strayed from this original humanitarian gesture, the existence of compensatory education would be understandable. However, educators soon equated physical deprivation with cultural deprivation. "While we must not confuse biological deprivation with cultural deprivation, there is little doubt that very frequently the two are associated . . . "[9] Accordingly, they developed a specialized language to categorize those whom they proposed to compensate:

> "Culturally deprived, culturally impoverished, educationally retarded, economically impoverished, culturally disadvantaged, chronically poor, educational deprived, culturally alienated, *ad infinitum* . . . "[10]

The term "compensatory" came later—perhaps to cover a multitude of sins.

While the devastating effects of poverty cannot be belittled, the confusion between physical and cultural needs must be questioned. This confusion is best revealed within the specialized language; in particular, the indiscriminate use of three phrases: "educationally retarded", "economically impoverished" and "culturally deprived"—in that order. Inherent in this jargon is an underlying assumption that failure in school must mean poverty at home which usually means cultural deprivation (whatever cultural deprivation means). Another point which should be made is that there are significant differences involved with regard to doing badly in school, being poor and having no culture. Undoubtedly all three factors may be interrelated, but not necessarily. And those who take for granted that they are related have a fuzzy knowledge of the meaning of culture.

The term has various meanings, all of which usually carry positive connotations. In the Anglo-Saxon context, people are often referred to as "cultured" when they are endowed with Emily Post manners and social graces, or when they appreciate the world of fine arts. To call someone "uncultured" is to insult him.

However, sociologically speaking, culture simply means the way of life of a people. When sociologists and anthropologists speak of culture, they mean value systems, social structures, customs and traditions, elements which pervade all societies. It follows that all people have a culture, a way of life, a life-style. And different peoples have different life-styles. And people with little money and few material possessions usually have a culture, too. To associate physical deprivation with cultural deprivation is to imply that poor people are void of social mores, norms, values, rituals and traditions. Some poor people may suffer from normlessness under any cultural context, but in most cases this implication is simply not true.

There is yet a deeper issue underlying this discussion and that is the hidden meaning of compensatory education. Since there is no easy way to open the subject, let's start by asking more questions. If we agree that "culture" means a way of life, then "cultural deprivation" means deprivation from a life-style. But whose life-style? Deprivation in relation to whose culture? Whose values, traditions, structures and so on?

When compensatory educators employ their jargon, they are doing so in relationship to middle-class values because middle-class standards are used as criteria from which the children are judged. Consider the following statement:

> "As the child attempts to communicate with others, and especially with his parents, he uses a relatively crude and limited language. In many middle-class homes the child's language is extended by the parent's response to his statements and questions. In culturally deprived homes, the parent is more likely to respond to the child with a monosyllable or to nod the head without using any words. The point of this is that one major difference between culturally deprived and more advantaged homes is the extension and development of the speech of children".[11]

There seems to be a blanket assumption that only a middle-class home is capable of providing perceptual, linguistic and intellectual development in children.[12] This assumption ignores the fact that children can develop perception, language and intelligence within their own cultural contexts, apart from middle-class homes.

It is true that children may do badly in school because of culture, not necessarily because they are bereft of culture or because their culture is inferior, but rather because it is different from the one propagated in school. Specifically, in Canada about 90% of the Native children either fail and/or drop out of school, not because they are "culturally impoverished" (although many suffer from physical want), but because in most cases their backgrounds are not middle-class. Most schools in North America are middle-class oriented and the teachers, teaching methods and curriculum naturally patronize middle-class children. The school system is so built that it often cannot relate or respond to children whose backgrounds do not subscribe to the middle-class culture. The concept of compensatory education was born partly in recognition of this, except in a backward sort of fashion; that is, since one cannot blame the children for being "retarded", "disadvantaged" or "impoverished", one compensates them for it. But is it really the children who need to be compensated? Apart from obvious physical need, is it the children who are deprived? Rather, could it not be that the school system and society itself is "disadvantaged"? Why are children and their parents the first to be stigmatized when perhaps, in fact, it is the institution that may be failing them? Of course, a fundamental question is being raised. Does the school exist for the child, or is the child to conform to the set patterns and expectations of the school?

This question may not be so crucial to groups of people whose families and school systems nourish each other. But it is important to people whose familial structures, educational outlooks and priorities vary from the dominant expectations. Perhaps the matter should be equally important to educators who believe in the ideals of democracy, pluralism and personal freedom.

The meaning of compensatory education is directly related to the meaning found in history books. Just as the ancient Indian was termed savage largely because he stood in the way of European expansionism, a Native child today is often considered deprived because his values may not relate to the modern concept of "progress". In other words, compensatory education as revealed in analysis of its jargon is no less ethnocentric than the philosophy expressed in history books. In fact, it is more insidious because it is couched under the pretext of liberalism and service to mankind, "mankind" most often meaning minority groups. And ironically, at the very time that low income youth was being classified as culturally deprived, middle-class youth was floundering its way into Yorkville, en masse.

3. Beyond Words

The written word has done its part in demeaning Indian people, and fortunately, it is beginning to receive critical attention. However, the attitudes, ideas and images those words sought to convey are still being transmitted into new mediums such as moving and still pictures.

As if to carry on the tradition of history books, Hollywood movies, especially Westerns, have grossly distorted the Indian image. However, these "dusters" carry the distinction of at least recognizing that the Indian had a viable language of his own. The Indian could say "How" and "Ugh". And in his more verbose moments, he could also comment, "Heap Big Chief", or "Me pow wow". Why, the Native was almost talkative—thanks to Hollywood!

Probably more than any other medium, Hollywood westerns have used the least amount of factual material with the wildest imagination. And Hollywood has successfully evaded its societal responsibilities under the guise of art and entertainment, perhaps because the public (including many Native people) has swallowed every inch of the "great silver screen".

Beyond secular movies, there are "educational" films about Indians in classrooms. Throughout my school years I remember seeing more films on Eskimos than on Indians, and none whatsoever on the Métis. And all I remember about the ones on Indians was that Indians were shown as buffalo hunters, construction workers, rodeo riders and fire fighters. I especially recall a film, because I saw it only about five times, extolling Indians as height-lovers. Accordingly, the camera followed an Indian man as he climbed up, up, up through the troposphere, the ionosphere—and finally, the man reached what seemed to

60 Defeathering the Indian

To dwell on the past, on poverty, or on the rural aspects of Native housing alone is to preserve the old stereotypes. The modern photograph at the right provides a necessary balance and perspective to the stereotyped image depicted in the one above.

be the stratosphere. And from that outer space the camera dizzily zoomed down to earth. And I, not having the constitution to brave the skies where angels fear to tread, found myself clutching at my desk! No one explained to me that these were the Mohawks and I, a Cree Métis, was free to remain skeptical of the stratosphere!

Illustrations and pictures in school textbooks are also powerful tools in preserving stereotypes. With regard to pictorial stereotypes of Indians, researchers analyzing Ontario textbooks in 1971 found the following:

> In general Indians emerged as the least favored of all the groups. An overwhelming number were portrayed as primitive and unskilled; not infrequently they were shown as aggressive and hostile as well. Although most have worn western dress for generations, 95 percent were shown in tribal dress or only partly clothed. In 86 percent of the illustrations, one or more Indian males were shown wearing feathers or feathered headdresses. Admittedly, many of the texts we examined were history texts dealing with a bygone era, but this would not explain why so few were shown in western dress, why many were shown naked or half naked (the climate and therefore the winter season in Canada has been relatively constant during the years of our written history), and why *none* were shown in skilled or professional occupations.[13]

At the moment there is a 1972 publication floating around waiting to be used as a social studies text. Unfortunately, its pages are full of pictorial stereotypes. Its illustrations highlight two standard portrayals of Indians; either the Indians are covered with feathers, or they are not covered at all! Also, in each case, they are either "lurking" or warring.

In the Context of the Classroom:

About history books

Most of us are not brave enough to burn history books that are outrightly discriminatory. Even if we were, we would be faced with a new problem—many empty shelves in our libraries! Besides, such history books have already spread their gospel.

However, just because we cannot destroy these books does not mean we have to accept them uncritically. We can learn to read them with perspective. We can teach students to become literary critics.

In relation to Indians we can teach at least the following things about history books.

"Back to Batoche", an annual event for Métis people, in celebration of being Métis

a. Unfairness can occur in the use of language. Words describing Indians consistently have negative connotations while those used for the writer's group have favorable connotations. For example, the Indians were often "lurking" while the cowboys were "scouting". The Indians "murdered" while the others "killed".
   Another more modern form of discriminatory word usage is to say that Indians are exclusively "problems" or "angry militants".
b. Unfairness occurs through neglecting to provide up-to-date material.
c. Unfairness occurs through deleting significant aspects of Indian history, such as the annihilation of the Beothuk tribe.
d. Unfairness occurs by pointing out all of the Indian's faults while extolling the virtues of the writer's group.
e. Unfairness occurs by giving superficial and token treatment to the Indian's contributions to the North American culture.
f. Unfairness occurs by printing only one side of the story.

We can teach students to read their material in context. We can explain to them the mood and beliefs of the times, when Indians were termed savages. As an example we can explain that much of the material about Louis Riel was written when he was most hated and feared. We can call attention to the fact that since most whites could not understand any Indian languages, they could not adequately write about the ways of the Indians.

How about the word "primitive"? The word is a value judgement and has, at best, pejorative connotations. In school many of my social studies classes invariably started off with a discussion on "primitive man". And just as invariably, North and South American Indians, Eskimos, Australian Maoris, African aborigines, and so forth were used as examples. But I do not recall much, if any, reference to the primitive days of Europe. I did not learn of their cave dwellings and huts, nor of their flake tools and wax tablets. I did not learn that in the 1600's the people of Northern Scotland and Ireland had no plows and used bows and arrows. I did not learn that they had treaties with the English, who outlawed their use of whiskey and guns and even their languages. Instead I learned about glorified castles, ingenious moats, and kings and lords. I learned that the English were a gallant, adventuresome, conquering people. For a long time, I think I believed that the white man was born with wings. Angelic ones at that!

If we must teach about "primitive man" then <u>let us at least teach that no one of us has escaped primitiveness</u>.

Furthermore, in the teachers' haste to use Indians as specimens of primitivity, they forgot to tell us about the Iroquois' mature and workable political system, about Indian architecture, about the Northwest Coast Indians' masterful achievements in sculpture or the brilliant beadwork of the Plains Indians, and so on and on. Not until I was in junior high school did I learn anything about the Mayan, Aztec and Inca empires. However, I do believe that Native Studies are now beginning to receive better treatment in schools.

About compensatory education

The discussion on compensatory education probably applies more to policy makers and administrators in various bureaucracies than it does to teachers. Nonetheless, teachers have been influenced by the specialized language in several ways; their expectations of Native children remain low, and they often accept the terminology and its implications without question.

It has been my impression in the last several years that many teachers have bent over backwards for their Native charges. They have done so with good intentions, which is praiseworthy. And to be sure, working with Native children with extra care and patience has probably been warranted in some cases.

Still, treating these children so specially that they are set apart from other students is an indication of something besides good-heartedness. It reflects having low expectations of them as a group, and failing to see them as individuals. It is not trusting them to be competent on their own.

But really, what else can teachers think when they are fed with such phrases as "chronically poor" or "educationally retarded"? There are

The first house completed under the Métis Housing Program (co-ordinated by the Alberta Housing Corporation) is officially handed over to a family.

rarely terms more fatalistic than "chronic" and "retarded"! Such a mental set leaves little room for children to call forth their individual capabilities, resources and skills.

A personal essay on poverty

Liberalism has made much of poverty in our last decade. Statistics on poverty have been flying around from all directions. And as I mentioned before, Native people have been closely associated with it; so closely in fact that some very significant questions have been bypassed.

What is poverty anyway? Is it the failure to reach beyond that magical Poverty Line established by the Economic Council of Canada? Or is it "... relative to the living standard the rest of society enjoys".[14] And more important, what is so sacred about what the majority enjoys?

To me it seems obvious that poverty is relative all right; but not necessarily relative to the wealth of the majority, but rather to one's own perceptions of his material possessions.

My two brothers, one sister and I grew up in a one-roomed but well-managed log cabin. Many of our clothes were handsewn by my very resourceful mother. All our wooden furniture (two beds, one table, a cupboard, several night stands, three chairs and a bench) was put together by my practical father. Our diet consisted of a large variety of wild meats, berries, bannock, potatoes, some vegetables and herbal teas and so on, all of which were usually cooked with originality and imagination.

At the age of nine, against my father's perceptive advice, I howled my way into school. He knew only too well that sooner or later I would come home with new desires. As predicted, a few months later I wanted juicy red apples, oranges, bananas, trembling jello, bread and even red-and-white striped toothpaste! Once, my father teasingly wondered what I could possibly do with toothpaste and brush because my teeth were all falling out! Toothless or not, I found the pictures at school powerfully suggestive.

Other school pictures also played with my mind. I saw Dick, Jane and Sally's suburban home and their grandparent's expansive and, oh, so clean farm. Not for a long time was I to appreciate my home again.

The point is, I had been perfectly content to sleep on the floor, eat rabbit stew and read and play cards by kerosene lamp until my perceptions were swayed at school. Neither had I suffered spiritual want. I had been spellbound by my mother's ability to narrate Cree legends and enriched by my father's dreams, until the teacher outlawed Cree and made fun of dreams.

From then on I existed in poverty; not with reference to our log cabin, our food and our small wood-stove as compared to the brick schoolhouse, its food and its huge, coal-burning pot-belly stove, but because I was persuaded by my teacher's propaganda and the pictures.* The teacher's authoritarianism, coupled with his failure to reinforce whatever world we came from, effectively weakened our respect for our parents.

Still, there is more to poverty than its relativity. Even if I had believed in my home and its simple beauties, it is true that I had no money. And without that commodity, eventually I could not be mobile. And to be immobile in any society is to be quite choiceless. It is at this point that equal opportunity becomes meaningless.

It is psychologically cathartic to know that one has a choice with his existence. Ultimately, poverty in the North American context is not having enough money to choose among alternatives. Poverty exacts its toll on people not always because of a mere lack of material possessions, but often because of choicelessness.

Today, there are hundreds of urban dwellers who are suffering from "cabinitis". Come Friday afternoon there is a mass and speedy exodus to the "simple" life of their cabins. These people are often happy there because they are there by choice. They feel a sense of self-direction.

People may be "culturally deprived" perhaps only in that they are

---

* It must be said that this teacher meant well. He was by nature a disciplinarian but not malicious. Apparently, he sincerely believed that his ways were for the good of the Native children.

Graduation Day, an important step toward equal opportunity

deprived of choice. In this sense then, most of us are "culturally deprived" in some area because most of us cannot choose everything we want out of life.

Now I live in a city, and I often see children playing on concrete, at artificial playgrounds and in overcrowded parks or swimming pools. I always feel a profound sense of sadness that these children cannot have what I had as a child. No spruce branch from which to master a Tarzanian swing. No soft moss to land on if you fall. No moonlight rendezvous beside a creek, watching a beaver tirelessly build his dam. No place to build an honest-to-goodness, creaking, but functioning, ferris wheel! No pond or lake or river to try out a self-made raft, row boat or canoe. Or to skinny-dip in. No green space to just run and run and run. No wooded meadow in which to lie and sleepily feel akin to the lethargic clouds. No crocuses, wild roses, tiger lilies or bluebells to sniff.

Cultural deprivation?

Yes, we must work towards equal opportunity for all. We must help people reach a sense of self-direction and mobility. We must lift people to the place of choice. But we cannot, we must not, dictate what people should choose.

Beyond words

At first glance it seems that the effects of secular movies are entirely beyond the control of classrooms, but this is not necessarily so. We can teach students to become movie critics just as we can teach them to be literary critics. Beyond that, we can make sure that our classrooms have sufficient accurate information to counteract, if necessary, what is seen on the screens.

Pictorial stereotypes are a thorny problem, too, and they do not seem to prickle the sensibilities of so many people. They float absolutely everywhere: in comic strips, comic books, history books, novels, paintings, cartoons and even on billboards.

Perhaps the best that teachers can do is to openly discuss pictorial stereotypes and expose them wherever they can be found.

5
Miscellaneous Reflections

While I was unearthing material for this handbook, I found some intriguing *and* surprising "information" about Native students. Two things in particular caught my attention.

Apparently in all kindness, one handbook cautioned teachers never to praise any Indian students in her classroom. Praise is not the Indian way, the handbook said. It would alienate the Indian student from his Indian peer group.

Another handbook expostulated on why Indian students avoid eye contact with teachers. Never fear, the handbook counselled, this is only a traditional sign of respect!

If these two sweeping generalizations were not so pathetic, I would not have stopped laughing. Perhaps there are some Indian tribes with such characteristics, although I am not aware of any. I do know that I have never met a Native individual who spurned genuine praise. I know also that in any classroom, white, Indian or mixed, a teacher's praise can alienate any student from his peer group.

In my elementary grades I, along with many other Native students, avoided my teachers' eyes not because of respect, but out of fear. When I reached junior high school and for the first time respected a teacher, I no longer habitually counted my toes.

Where does one draw the line between judging a person as an individual and as a cultural entity? To be sure, it is not always easy, for each individual is a product of his environment. Yet it seems to me that there comes a time when we must recognize each person as an individual rather than as a carbon copy of what we suppose to be his culture. For within one's cultural context, one varies from others of his culture in his expressions, creativity and feelings. Personally, I think people are like snowflakes; they all differ from one another.

Most individuals belong to groups and groups differ from each other because of the variables of tradition, geography and physical make-up. While we acknowledge distinguishing characteristics in groups, we must ultimately judge a person on his own merits.

In my mind there is no conflict between an individual and his culture. If we maintain respect and dignity for personhood as a guiding principle in any interaction, there is little that can go wrong, apart from social embarrassment, which is usually forgivable. For if we

" . . . it seems to me that there comes a time when we must recognize each person as an individual rather than as a carbon copy of what we suppose to be his culture . . . Personally, I think people are like snowflakes; they all differ from one another."

respect an individual, we are not likely to demean his environment. And if perchance his environment is less than favorable (e.g. people indoctrinated with Nazism), we can still treat his person with dignity.

It seems that we are ever tempted to diverge into two extremes; we dwell upon our differences to the point of excluding our similarities, or we universalize everyone at the expense of identity and diversity.

It appears to me that many kind, decent and capable but frustrated teachers are susceptible to the latter. Teachers are subjected to all sorts of conflicting messages and confusing data. They are faced with parental demands, staff and student idiosyncrasies and curriculum overloads. At the same time there are many voices pushing to be heard. It is understandable that many throw up their hands in resignation. It is then easy to rationalize, "We're all the same anyway" and to continue on the path of dominant conventions.

Yet, it is at this point that we must question universalization. If conformity is adopted as a rule of life, to whose standards do we conform? We are back to the question of different values, social structures and perceptions.

Beyond this, uniformity risks global boredom. What could we possibly do without variety?

Sensing a rapid trend towards ostensibly middle-class homogeneity in schools, some enlightened educators have plunged into Intercultural Education—the guardian of diversity. Intercultural Education is a relatively new thing in Canada, and its initial focus has been on Native Studies. French, Ukrainian and Hutterite studies are also in the embryonic stages of development.

The intentions of developing this new curriculum are commendable, and certainly healthy. As I understand it, they seek to bring various ethnic groups and their contributions to their rightful places in Canada. In turn, this enriches the students' experiences in school.

However, Intercultural Education can unwittingly become a tool of separation and schism. Unfortunately, it happens so often that while groups are eager to be heard and represented in schools, they are not so enthusiastic to share the platform, especially in funding!

Also, Intercultural Education is vulnerable to exhausting its energies upon differences, which can be another vehicle of fragmentation.

How do we bring together peoples of different races, different lifeviews, different languages and various preferences and keep them together? How do we build up one group of people without degrading others? Let me go off on a brief and perhaps visionary tangent.

- If anything or anyone different from dominant expectations were studied, if studied at all, with more than fringe interest;
- If all curriculum materials and textbooks were radically renewed with a view towards objectivity, depth and fairness to all peoples;
- If from Kindergarten to University, students were consistently taught that different values, religions and systems exist and that each is viable within the context of its people, era and location;
- If peoples from non-Western, non-white, non-Christian and non-capitalist backgrounds were treated without condemnation by implication (by extolling white Anglo-Saxon virtues at the exclusion of others);
- If Native, Black, Oriental and other ethnic peoples of Canada received more than superficial, token and peripheral attention in classrooms;
- If it were a given thing that all these "ifs" were a daily reality in our classrooms, then I doubt that we would need Intercultural Education as such. School itself would be intercultural education.

Neither would we be uninformed enough to lump everybody into one pot. We would learn to acknowledge diversity without feelings of insecurity, for each of us would be duly recognized and respected.

Really, such dreams should neither be strange nor impossible in a land that boasts of a cultural mosaic, enlightenment, pluralism and democracy. But it does take time and effort to make dreams come true. The sooner we start, the better.

So be it!

FOOTNOTES

Chapter 2
1. In his study, "Grade Placement of Northern Alberta Métis Pupils, 1969 and 1970", Dr. J.W. Chalmers used *economic status* as one of the criteria for defining the Métis. (Unpublished paper, Edmonton, 1970). Some of the statistics from this study are included in *Education Behind the Buckskin Curtain* by Chalmers.
2. John Collier, *Indians of the Americas* (New York: New American Library, Inc., 1947), p. 27.
3. For copies of treaties see, Coles Canadiana Collection, *Indian Treaties and Surrenders* (Toronto: Coles, 1973); Morris Alexander, *The Treaties of Canada With the Indians* (Toronto: Coles, 1971); and Kent Gooderham, *The Days of the Treaties* (Toronto: Griffin House, 1972).
4. The various contributions made by Métis people are well presented in an unpublished paper, "Indigenous Human Capital in the Economic History of Canada" by Isaac N. Glick (Unpublished paper, Edmonton). See also, Joseph Kinsey Howard, *Strange Empire* (Toronto: Swan Publishing, 1952), Chapter 1.
5. Joseph Kinsey Howard, *Strange Empire*, (Toronto: Swan Publishing, 1952), pp. 314-315. See also Maria Campbell, *Halfbreed* (Toronto: McClelland and Stewart Limited, 1973), Introductory Remarks.
6. Gerald Tailfeathers is from the Blood Reserve at Cardston, Alex Janvier is a Chipewyan from Cold Lake, Henry Nanooch is from Fox Lake and Sarain Stump was originally an Albertan but he is presently employed by the Saskatchewan Indian Cultural College at Saskatoon. Ron Hamilton is from British Columbia, Allen Sapp is from Saskatchewan, Jackson Beardy is from Manitoba, and Daphne "Odjig" Beavon, Norval Morrisseau (Ojibway) and Lloyd Caibaiosai are all from Ontario.
7. Vine Deloria, Jr., *God is Red* (New York: Grosset & Dunlap, Inc., 1974).

Chapter 3
1. John Collier, *Indians of the Americas* (New York: New American Library, Inc., 1947), p. 131.
2. Claude Aubry, *Agouhanna* (Toronto: Doubleday (Canada) Limited, 1972), p. 8.
3. Aubry, *Agouhanna*, p. 63.
4. Shelia Burnford, *Without Reserve* (Toronto: McClelland and Stewart Limited, 1969), p. 224.
5. For further discussion of the slaughter of the buffalo see Joseph Kinsey Howard, *Strange Empire* (Toronto: Swan Publishing, 1952)
6. "The Other Side", *The Christian Leader*, July 10, 1973.
7. Dee Brown, *Bury My Heart At Wounded Knee* (New York: Holt, Rinehart & Winston, 1970), p. 134.

Chapter 4
1. John Collier, *Indians of the Americas* (New York: New American Library, Inc., 1947) p. 113.
2. *Ibid.*
3. Vine Deloria, Jr., *Custer Died for Your Sins* (New York: Macmillan Co., 1969). p. 14.
4. Dee Brown. *Bury My Heart At Wounded Knee* (New York: Holt, Rinehart & Winston, 1970), p. 89.
5. Garnet McDiarmid and David Pratt, *Teaching Prejudice* (Toronto: Ontario Institute for Studies in Education, 1971), p. 91.
6. Benjamin S. Bloom and others, *Compensatory Education for Cultural Deprivation* (New York: Holt, Rinehart & Winston, 1968) p. 8.
7. *Ibid.*
8. *Ibid.*, p. 10.
9. *Ibid.*, p. 9.
10. Herbert A. Callihoe, "A Rationale for Compensatory Education in The Public Schools of the Province of Alberta", (Unpublished paper for Department of Education, Alberta, 1972).
11. Bloom, *op. cit.*, p. 14 (A crucial point here, also, is *whose* speech are we to extend and develop? This question becomes poignantly relevant in Canada where we have a multi-language situation).
12. *Ibid.*, pp. 12-16.
13. McDiarmid and Pratt, *op. cit.*, p. 51.
14. Ian Adams and others, *The Real Poverty Report* (Edmonton: Hurtig Publishers, 1971), p. 8.

RECOMMENDATIONS FOR FURTHER READING

Chapter 2
On Treaties.
Canada: Department of Indian Affairs and Northern Development. *Indian Policy.* Ottawa: Queen's Printer, 1969.
Cardinal, Harold. *The Unjust Society.* Edmonton: Hurtig Publishers, 1969.
Dempsey, Hugh. *Crowfoot.* Edmonton: Hurtig Publishers, 1972.
Indian Chiefs of Alberta. *Citizens Plus.* Edmonton: Indian Association of Alberta, 1970.

On the Métis.
Campbell, Maria. *Halfbreed.* Toronto: McClelland and Stewart Limited, 1973.
Howard, Joseph Kinsey. *Strange Empire.* Toronto: Swan Publishing, 1952.
Lusty, Terrance. *Louis Riel: Humanitarian.* Calgary: Métis Historical Society, 1972.
Lusty, Terrance. *Métis: Social-Political Movement.* Calgary: Métis Historical Society, 1973.

On Art.
Dockstader, Frederick J. *Indian Art in North America.* Toronto: McClelland and Stewart Limited, 1961.

On Relgion and Values.
Black Elk. *Black Elk Speaks.* As told to John C. Neihardt. Lincoln: University of Nebraska Press, 1961.
Black Elk. *The Sacred Pipe: Black Elk's Account of the Seven Rites of The Oglala Sioux.* As told to Joseph Epes Brown. Baltimore: Penguin, 1971.
Deloria, Vine, Jr. *God Is Red.* New York: Grosset & Dunlap, Inc., 1974.
McLuhan, T.C. (ed.). *Touch the Earth.* Toronto: New Press, 1971.
Seton, Ernest T. and Julia M. Seton. *The Gospel of the Red Man.* Santa Fe: Seton Village, 1963.
Storm, Hyemeyohsts. *Seven Arrows.* New York: Harper & Row, 1972.

On Current Issues and Problems (Native Newspapers).
It is highly desirable that every school receive one or two Native newspapers, in order that students and teachers have easy access to them.
As a matter of interest, one of the latest tallies of Native-oriented periodicals has yielded the following figures:

Ontario	35	Northwest Territories	7
British Columbia	17	Quebec	4
Manitoba	14	New Brunswick	3
Alberta	12	Yukon Territory	2
Saskatchewan	9	Nova Scotia	1

Recommended Native newspapers include:
Kainai News. (bi-weekly, $5.00/yr) Indian News Media, Box 808, Cardston, Alberta. Editor: Caen Bly.
The Native People. (weekly, $10.00/yr.) Alberta Native Communications Society, 11427 Jasper Avenue, Edmonton, Alberta. Editor: George LeFleur; Assistant Editor: Wendy Gray.
Manitoba Métis Federation News. (monthly, $3.00/yr) Manitoba Métis Federation News, 301 - 374 Donald Street, Winnipeg, Manitoba. Editor: John P. Burelle; Assistant Editor: Barbara A. Bruce.
The Saskatchewan Indian. (monthly, $5.00/yr.) The Saskatchewan Indian, 1114 Central Avenue, Prince Albert, Saskatchewan. Editor: Lucille Bell; Editorial Board: David Ahenakew, Cliff Starr, John Ursan.

Chapter 3
Alberta Human Rights Commission, 10808 - 99 Avenue, Edmonton, Alberta (The Commission has a number of pamphlets and newsletters).
Canada: Department of Indian Affairs and Northern Development, *Let's Take A Look at Prejudice and Discrimination: A Study Guide.* Ottawa: Queen's Printer, 1970.
McDiarmid, Garnet and David Pratt, *Teaching Prejudice.* Toronto: Ontario Institute for Studies in Education, 1971.

Chapter 4
Adams, Ian, and others. *The Real Poverty Report.* Edmonton: Hurtig Publishers, 1971.
Bloom, Benjamin S. and others. *Compensatory Education for Cultural Deprivation.* New York: Holt, Rinehart & Winston, 1965.
Brown, Dee. *Bury My Heart At Wounded Knee.* New York: Holt Rinehart & Winston, 1970.
Deloria, Vine, Jr. *Custer Died for Your Sins.* New York: Macmillan Co., 1969.
Simon, Arthur. *Faces of Poverty.* London: Collier-Macmillan, 1966.